FIRST STEPS

FIRST STEPS

Paul J. Loth

Illustrated by
Daniel J. Hochstatter

THOMAS NELSON PUBLISHERS
Nashville

Published in Nashville, Tennessee, by Oliver-Nelson Books, a division of Thomas Nelson, Inc., Publishers, and distributed in Canada by Lawson Falle, Ltd., Cambridge, Ontario.

The Bible version used in this publication is THE NEW KING JAMES VERSION. Copyright © 1979, 1980, 1982, Thomas Nelson, Inc., Publishers.

Printed in the United States of America.

Library of Congress Cataloging-in-Publication Data

Loth, Paul J.
　　First steps / Paul J. Loth.
　　　　p.　　cm.
　　Summary: Four-step family devotions which involve thinking about life situations, listening to Bible stories, discussion of spiritual ideas, and prayer.
　　ISBN 0-8407-9167-4
　　1. Children—Prayer-books and devotions—English.　2. Children—Religious life. [1. Prayer books and devotions. 2. Christian life.] I. Title.
BV4870.L68　1992
242'.62—dc20
　　　　　　　　　　　　　　　　　　　　　　　　　　　92-11389
　　　　　　　　　　　　　　　　　　　　　　　　　　　　CIP
　　　　　　　　　　　　　　　　　　　　　　　　　　　　AC

2　3　4　5　6　—　97　96　95　94　93　92

Contents

Tips for Living for God

God Is The Greatest

An Open Letter to Parents

I know from personal experience with my children that family devotions can be a burden or a blessing—or both!

When family devotions are successfully implemented, they can be the most blessed time of the day. They provide the quality time with our children we so desire, and we as parents have the rare opportunity to pass along our spiritual insights and love for the Lord.

A Bible verse that best summarizes the teaching of each lesson is included at the end. Continue to use this verse when appropriate in daily discussions with your children to reinforce the lesson. Several significant activities are usually involved. These elements have been included in each devotional in this book.

The Thinking Step: Jesus always started His lessons by making people think about their life situations. When family devotional times begin with a moment to reflect on life, the Bible story takes on special meaning.

The Listening Step: Romans 10:17 asserts, "Faith comes by hearing, and hearing by the word of God." God's Word will not return to us void. That is why the stories included in this devotional book are Bible stories. The Lord uses every Bible story in the lives of children. The pictures in this book accompany the Bible stories in The Listening Step and will be meaningful to your children.

Children always ask "so what?" That question needs to be answered to their satisfaction. Only then will the Bible story and the spiritual teaching take effect in their young lives.

The Talking Step: Talking during family devotional times should be more than a review of Bible facts. Talking should involve honest questions about spiritual truths and application to real-life situations. The questions in this section will promote these kinds of family discussions.

The Praying Step: God describes Himself as a loving father who is concerned about every detail of our lives. Teach your children to pray with that in mind, as they would converse with you, their parents. This section includes points of prayer rather than prayers to read or repeat.

One more thought. I have discovered that setting aside a consistent time for family devotions is perhaps the greatest key to their success. So find a time free of distractions and scheduling conflicts.

May the quality time with your children be a time of blessing and result in the spiritual growth of all members of your family.

Paul J. Loth, Ed.D.

God Wants Us to Be Happy

Genesis 1:1–19

The Thinking Step

- Do you want to be happy? Why?
- Do you want your brothers and sisters and your friends to be happy? Why?
- Do you think God wants you to be happy? Why?

The Listening Step

God wants us to be happy. God wants us to be happy so much that He made a beautiful world for us. He wants us to live and play in it and be happy. God wants us to enjoy everything in the world.

God first made the sky. God filled the sky with the sun, the stars, and the moon so we can enjoy daytime and nighttime. He also made the land and the ocean so we can have fun on dry ground and in the water. God made the ground very pretty with flowers, trees, and beaches. He gave us a beautiful place to live. God wants us to be happy.

The Talking Step

- What is your favorite thing about the world?
- Why do you think God made it?

The Praying Step
- Thank God for making such a beautiful world.
- Thank God for loving you.

In the beginning God created the heavens and the earth.
—*Genesis 1:1*

God Thinks of Everything

Genesis 1—2

The Thinking Step

- Have you ever thought about how your body was made?
- Every part of your body has a purpose. You have what you need to do whatever you want to do.

The Listening Step

God made the world. He made the world exactly the way He wanted and filled it with animals and birds. And then He made people.

First, He made a man. God gave him eyes to see all the beautiful things in the world. God gave him ears to hear all the beautiful sounds in the world. God gave him a nose to smell all the interesting smells in the world. God gave him hands and fingers to hold and feel all the beautiful things in the world. God also gave the man two legs and two feet so he could walk and enjoy many, many things. God even showed the man all the animals and let him pick a name for each one.

But God knew the man should not be alone. God made a woman to keep the man from being alone.

The Talking Step

- Why did God make us?
- Why did God make both man and woman?
- What is special about how we were made?

12

The Praying Step

- Thank God for making you.
- Thank God for thinking of everything to give you a happy life.

Then God saw everything that He had made, and indeed it was very good.

—*Genesis 1:31*

Happiness Comes from Obeying God

Genesis 3

The Thinking Step

- Do you ever disobey your mom or dad?
- How do you feel when you disobey?
- Are you happy or unhappy?

The Listening Step

God wanted all of us to be happy. He made a beautiful world for us. God wanted Adam and Eve to be happy. He let them live in the beautiful Garden of Eden.

There was everything in the Garden of Eden to make Adam and Eve happy. There were plants and trees. There was water. There were animals. But God said to Adam and Eve, "Do not eat from the tree of the knowledge of good and evil."

Adam and Eve did not obey that rule. Both Adam and Eve ate from the tree.

What happened? Adam and Eve had to leave the beautiful garden. God punished them for the rest of their lives.

The Talking Step

- Why do you think Adam and Eve disobeyed God?
- What would have happened if they had continued obeying God?
- What happens to us if we do what pleases God?

The Praying Step

- Thank God for caring for us.
- Thank God for wanting us to be happy.
- Ask God to help you obey Him.

You shall walk after the LORD your God and fear Him, and keep His commandments and obey His voice; you shall serve Him and hold fast to Him.

—Deuteronomy 13:4

Jesus Takes Care of Us

Mark 4:35–41

The Thinking Step
- What scares you?
- What do you do when you are scared?

The Listening Step

Jesus and the disciples were in a boat. Jesus was tired, so He went to sleep. While He was sleeping, the wind started to blow. Then it blew harder. The wind blew the waves over the sides of the boat.

Jesus was still sleeping. Finally, the disciples woke Him. "Do You not care that we are all going to die?" they said.

Jesus got up. He turned to the sky, looked at the high waves on the sea, and said, "Peace, be still!" Right away the wind and the high waves stopped.

The disciples were amazed! "Even the wind and the sea obey Him," they said. Jesus took care of the disciples. He was in control of everything all along.

The Talking Step
- Why do you think the wind and the high waves stopped when Jesus told them to stop?
- Do you think Jesus can take care of anything?

The Praying Step
- Think of something that scares you.
- Ask Jesus to take care of it.

Peace I leave with you, My peace I give to you.
—*John 14:27*

Jesus Died for You

Matthew 27:38–66

The Thinking Step

- Were you ever punished for something someone else did wrong?
- How did you feel?
- Would you ever ask to be punished instead of someone else? Why?

The Listening Step

We all have sin in us that makes us do bad things. We want to be good, but sometimes we are bad instead. The Bible calls that sin. We must be punished for our sins.

Jesus is God's Son. He never did anything wrong. He never sinned.

Jesus lived on earth a long, long time ago. He did not want us to be punished for our sins. So Jesus died for our sins. If we will believe in Jesus and ask Him to forgive us, He will!

The Talking Step

- Why should people believe in Jesus?
- What would happen if Jesus had not died for us?
- Have you ever asked Jesus to forgive you?

The Praying Step

- Thank Jesus for dying for you.
- Ask Him to forgive you and come into your life.
- Ask Jesus to help you tell others about Him.

> But God demonstrates His own love toward us, in that while we were still sinners, Christ died for us.
>
> —*Romans 5:8*

God Shares with Us

Luke 2:1–7

The Thinking Step

- What is your favorite toy or doll?
- How do you feel when someone plays with it?
- Would you ever give it away? Why?

The Listening Step

Mary and Joseph were on a long trip. They were very tired. Mary was especially tired because she was expecting her first child. They stopped at many hotels to find a room. But all the rooms were filled.

Joseph finally asked a hotel manager to let them sleep in the place where the animals stayed. That night Mary gave birth to her baby. His name was Jesus.

Jesus was God's only Son. God loved Jesus very much. Later God told everyone, "This is My Son whom I love. I am very proud of Him."

God did not want to give up His only Son. But there was no other way to save us. Because God loves us so much, He sent Jesus to earth.

The Talking Step

- What is the most important thing anyone ever gave you?
- How did it make you feel?
- What does God's giving up His Son, Jesus, tell us about how God feels about us?

The Praying Step

- Thank God for loving you.
- Thank God for sending Jesus.

For God so loved the world that He gave His only begotten Son, that whoever believes in Him should not perish but have everlasting life.

— John 3:16

Jesus Came for All of Us

Luke 2:8–14

The Thinking Step

- Did you ever meet someone important? Who?
- Was the person friendly to you?

The Listening Step

Shepherds take care of sheep. Some people do not think shepherds are important. But shepherds are important to God. Everyone is important to God.

God could have told the king that Jesus was coming. God could have told the businesspeople. God could have told the religious leaders. But He did not.

God told the shepherds. Why did He tell them? Because God wanted us to know that Jesus came for everyone.

The shepherds were watching their sheep in the fields. In the middle of the night, the dark sky got very bright (like it does during the day). An angel stood before the shepherds and said, "Do not be afraid! I bring you good news! Tonight your Savior is born in Bethlehem!" Then many angels filled the sky and praised God.

The Talking Step

- How would you have felt if you were one of the shepherds?
- Would you have been scared?
- How would it have made you feel to know that God told you first?

The Praying Step

- Thank Jesus for caring for you.
- Thank Jesus that He came to earth for all of us.
- Ask Jesus to help you tell your friends about Him.

Then the shepherds returned, glorifying and praising God for all the things that they had heard and seen, as it was told them.

—Luke 2:20

You Are Important to Jesus

Luke 15:3–6

The Thinking Step

- How would you feel if you lost one of your toys?
- Would you look for it, or would it not matter to you because you have other toys?

The Listening Step

Jesus told a story to His friends. The story was about a shepherd and his sheep. A shepherd is someone who takes care of sheep—like your mom or dad takes care of you.

The shepherd in Jesus' story is called the good shepherd. The good shepherd took care of 100 sheep. One day he was counting his sheep: ". . . 91, 92, 93, 94, 95, 96, 97, 98, 99 . . . 99 . . . 99 . . ." One sheep was missing!

What should he do? After all, he still had 99 safe. That was pretty good.

But the good shepherd loved all his sheep—every single one. So he went after the lost sheep. He looked everywhere and finally found it. The shepherd brought the lost sheep back safely.

Jesus cares for each one of us. We are all important to Him.

The Talking Step

- Would you have tried to find the lost sheep?
- What would God do if you stopped loving Him?

The Praying Step
- Thank Jesus for loving you.
- Thank Jesus that you are important to Him.

I say to you that likewise there will be more joy in heaven over one sinner who repents than over ninety-nine just persons who need no repentance.

—*Luke 15:7*

God Always Loves Us

Luke 15:11–24

The Thinking Step

- Did you ever do something so wrong to someone that you were afraid to see the person again?
- Did you think the person would ever forgive you?

The Listening Step

Jesus wants us to know that God loves us. God will always love us no matter what happens. Jesus told a story to help us know that God will never stop loving us.

A father had two sons. One son did not want to wait until he grew up to get his father's money. He wanted it now! To make his son happy, the father gave him the money.

The son had a great time! He had lots of friends and had a lot of fun. But soon he ran out of money. Then his friends left him. And he had no money left to buy food.

What should he do? He decided to go home. He would ask his father for a job. His father saw him coming and ran to meet him, welcoming him back with open arms.

The Talking Step

- How do you think God feels when we disobey Him and do wrong things?
- Do you think we could ever do something so wrong that God would not forgive us?
- If we do something wrong, what should we do?

The Praying Step
- Thank God for always loving you.
- Ask God to forgive you for wrong things you have done.
- Ask God to help you obey Him.

> For this my son was dead and is alive again; he was lost and is found.
>
> *—Luke 15:24*

Jesus Is Alive

Luke 24: 1–12

The Thinking Step

- Would you like to have a friend who was with you all the time?
- Would you like to have a friend who always helped you?
- Jesus is that friend.

The Listening Step

Mary Magdalene and several other women were sad. Jesus had died. They missed Jesus. They went to visit His grave. At the grave the women saw two angels. The angels told them, "Jesus is not here. Jesus is alive!"

Mary Magdalene and the other women were excited. They hurried to tell Jesus' friends. But Peter did not believe the women. Peter had to see for himself. He ran to the grave. It was true. Jesus was not there. Jesus was alive!

The Talking Step

- How would you feel if you were Mary Magdalene or one of the other women?
- What would you say to Jesus if you saw Him right now?

The Praying Step

- Thank Jesus for being alive.
- Thank Jesus for being with you all the time.
- Tell Jesus you are glad He is your friend.

He is not here, but is risen!   —*Luke 24:6*

God Accepts Everyone

Acts 10

The Thinking Step

- Are there people you do not like?
- Do you think there are people God does not like?
- Do you think there are people who are not acceptable to God?

The Listening Step

Peter loved God. He tried to make God happy. But Peter thought that only certain things and certain people were acceptable to God. God wanted to teach Peter to accept everyone.

One day Peter had a dream. He was hungry. He wanted something to eat. Down from heaven came food for him to eat. But it was not clean food. Peter said, "No. I would never eat anything that is unclean!" But God said, "What God has made clean you must never call unclean."

Peter thought about that. There were some people he thought were not acceptable to God. But if they were acceptable to God, he should accept them, too.

Just then three men came to the house. They asked for Peter. They wanted him to come with them. They wanted him to tell them more about God. The men were different from Peter. Peter had not thought they were acceptable to God. But now he knew God loved them. Peter accepted them, too.

The Talking Step

- What do you think Peter thought when the three men came to his house?
- What do you think about people who are different from you?
- Do you think God accepts them, too?

The Praying Step

- Ask God to help you accept people who are different from you.
- Thank God for accepting everyone.

> **Whoever fears Him and works righteousness is accepted by Him.**
>
> *—Acts 10:35*

Forgiveness Rather Than Fighting Back

Genesis 45:1–15

The Thinking Step

- When someone is mean to you, what do you want to do?
- What do you think would happen if you were nice to someone who was mean to you?

The Listening Step

Joseph's brothers were mean to him. His brothers were so mean that they sold Joseph as a slave to a man who lived far away.

God helped Joseph to become very important. One day, a long time later, Joseph's brothers came to him asking for help. But his brothers did not know who he was. What would Joseph do?

Joseph told everyone except his brothers to leave the room. He wanted to be alone with them. "I am your brother, Joseph," he told them. His brothers were scared. They thought Joseph would hurt them. Joseph said, "Do not be afraid. You meant to hurt me, but God used what you did to help me."

Joseph was nice to his brothers even though they had been mean to him.

The Talking Step

- How do you think Joseph's brothers felt?
- What would you have done if you were Joseph?
- How do you think God wanted Joseph to act?

The Praying Step

- Think of someone who has been mean to you.
- Ask God to help you forgive that person.
- Ask God to help you treat that person nicely.

You meant evil against me; but God meant it for good, in order to bring it about as it is this day, to save many people alive. Now therefore, do not be afraid; I will provide for you and your little ones.

—Genesis 50:20–21

Looking from the Inside Out

1 Samuel 16:1–13

The Thinking Step

- How do you pick your best friends?
- What is more important—how a person looks or how a person acts? Why?

The Listening Step

King Saul was not a good king anymore. He did not love God. King Saul did not obey God either. God told Samuel to find a new king for Israel.

Samuel visited Jesse and his family. Jesse showed Samuel seven of his sons. Samuel looked at Jesse's first son. *Certainly this is the one who will be the next king of Israel,* Samuel thought. But God said no. Samuel was looking at the outside of Jesse's sons. God was looking at the inside of each one—his heart. One by one, Samuel looked at each son. God said no each time.

"Are these all your sons?" Samuel asked Jesse.

"All except for David, my youngest son," Jesse answered. "He is watching the sheep."

"I would like to see him, too," Samuel said.

As soon as Samuel saw David, he knew David was God's choice to be king. David was a special servant of God.

The Talking Step

- Why did God pick David?
- How does what you are like on the inside make you act different?

The Praying Step

- Tell God you want to make Him happy.
- Ask God to help you do the right thing on the inside.

For man looks at the outward appearance, but the LORD looks at the heart.

—*1 Samuel 16:7*

A Friend Is Special

1 Samuel 18:1–4; 20:1–42

The Thinking Step

- Do you have a best friend?
- What makes that friend special?
- How do you treat your friend?
- How does your friend treat you?

The Listening Step

Jonathan and David were best friends. Jonathan was King Saul's son. King Saul thought David was his enemy. King Saul did not want Jonathan to be David's friend. Jonathan tried to find ways to help David.

Jonathan wanted his father and David to be friends. Jonathan even invited David to play music for the king. But King Saul tried to kill David!

Jonathan and David had one more idea for keeping their friendship. "I will go and talk to my father," Jonathan told David. "You wait outside. I will shoot three arrows, and I will send a young boy to find them. If I tell the boy, 'The arrows are beyond you,' it is still not safe for you and me to be friends."

Guess what happened? Jonathan shot the arrows. He told the boy, "Look, the arrows are beyond you." When David heard that, he was very sad because he and Jonathan were such good friends.

The Talking Step

- How do you know Jonathan and David were best friends?
- Do you think God was happy with the way David and Jonathan treated each other?
- How should you treat your friends?

The Praying Step

- Pray for your friends.
- Ask Jesus to help you be a good friend.

> Then Jonathan and David made a covenant, because he loved him as his own soul.
>
> —*1 Samuel 18:3*

Love Is Unselfish

1 Kings 3:16–28

The Thinking Step

- Name someone you love.
- Do you usually think of what is best for him or her or what is best for you?

The Listening Step

Two mothers had a problem. Both of them said they were the mother of one child. Only one could be the real mother, but neither woman would give up the baby.

King Solomon was very wise. The two mothers asked the king to decide who should keep the child. After King Solomon heard the problem, he thought for a moment. Then he told the mothers, "I think the only solution is to cut the child in half.

I will give one half of the child to each mother!"

One mother was shocked. "Do not do that!" she cried. "Give the child to the other mother if that is what it takes!"

"No," said King Solomon, "you are the real mother. You may keep your child." King Solomon knew that the real mother would be more concerned about her child's life than her own happiness.

The Talking Step

- How did King Solomon know the real mother?
- What would you have done if you were the mother?

The Praying Step
  • Ask God to help you be more concerned about others.

[Love] does not behave rudely, does not seek its own, is not provoked, thinks no evil.

—1 Corinthians 13:5

God Helps Those Who Obey Him

1 Kings 17:1–7

The Thinking Step

- Have you been punished for disobeying?
- Have you been punished for obeying?
- Do you remember a time when your brother, sister, or friend disobeyed, but you were good?
- Was the other person punished? Were you punished?

The Listening Step

King Ahab did not love God. King Ahab worshiped Baal instead. Baal was only a statue.

Elijah was God's prophet. Elijah loved God. He wanted people to obey God. He told people to obey God. But King Ahab did not listen to Elijah. The king would rather worship Baal.

God wanted the people to know that He is the only true God. So God told Elijah that He was not going to let it rain for a long time. Elijah told King Ahab what God said.

But the king still did not want to worship God.

God stopped the rain. But God took care of Elijah because he obeyed God. God told him to stay by a brook. Elijah drank water from the brook. God told special kinds of birds, ravens, to bring food to Elijah so he could eat.

God punished the people who did not obey Him. But God took care of Elijah because he obeyed God.

The Talking Step

- When you obey God, what happens?
- Does God take care of you?

The Praying Step

- Thank God for taking care of you when you obey Him.
- Ask God to help you obey Him.

Salvation belongs to the LORD.
Your blessing is upon Your people.
—*Psalm 3:8*

Giving All to Jesus

Mark 10:17–31

The Thinking Step

- Name someone or something that is very important to you.
- How much would you give up for that person or thing?
- What do you think your mom or dad would give up for you?

The Listening Step

A young man came to visit Jesus. The man loved Jesus very much.

"What do I need to do to have eternal life?" the man asked.

"You know what the Bible says," Jesus answered.

"Yes," the man said, "I have obeyed the Bible commands since I was a child."

"One more thing," Jesus said. "Sell everything you own. Then give the money to the poor and follow Me."

What should the man do? He was very rich.

The rich young man was very sad. He walked away from Jesus.

Jesus explained to the disciples, "It is hard for a rich man to go to heaven. But anyone who gives up things for Me will receive much more."

The Talking Step

- What would Jesus tell you to give up?
- What things would you have trouble giving up for Jesus?

The Praying Step
- Thank Jesus for dying and living again for you.
- Ask Jesus to tell you what you need to give up for Him.

And whatever you do in word or deed, do all in the name of the Lord Jesus.

—Colossians 3:17

Making Your Friends Happy

Luke 1:39–56

The Thinking Step

- When have you been really happy?
- Did you want to share your happiness with a special person? Who was it?
- How did that person help you be happy?

The Listening Step

Mary and Elizabeth were relatives. Elizabeth had been married a long time. But Mary was not yet married. Mary and Joseph were going to be married very soon. Both Elizabeth and Mary were very happy.

Elizabeth did not think she was going to have any children. She was very old. But God loved Elizabeth. God knew she wanted a baby. God wanted her to be happy. Soon Elizabeth would have a baby boy. The baby's name would be John. John would tell people about God.

Mary was going to have a baby, too. Mary's baby would be named Jesus. When Mary heard that Elizabeth was going to have a baby, she went to see her.

Elizabeth and Mary were together three months. Elizabeth helped Mary to be happy, and Mary helped Elizabeth to be happy.

The Talking Step

- Why do you think Mary and Elizabeth were together so long?
- Do you know someone you could help to be happy? How?

The Praying Step
- Ask God to help you make others happy.
- Thank God for giving you friends who can help you be happy.

Rejoice with those who rejoice. —*Romans 12:15*

Care About Everyone

Luke 5:27–32

The Thinking Step

- Do you like everyone?
- Do you know people who are not well liked by your friends?
- How do you think Jesus wants you to treat these people?

The Listening Step

Matthew was not well liked. In his job, he often cheated people. But Jesus made Matthew His friend anyway.

One day Matthew invited Jesus to his house to eat. Matthew also invited many of his other friends. These friends had the same job that Matthew had. They were not well liked either.

Jesus went to eat at Matthew's house.

Many people were surprised. They wanted to know why He was friends with Matthew. Do you know what Jesus said? "I want to spend time with people who do wrong things. They are the ones who need Me!"

Jesus cared about Matthew and his friends even though they did wrong things. We should care about everyone, too.

The Talking Step

- Do you think Jesus was right to eat with Matthew and his friends?
- Can you think of people you should be friends with?

The Praying Step
- Ask Jesus to help you be friends with people who are not well liked.
- Ask Jesus to give you chances to tell others about Him.

Therefore be merciful, just as your Father also is merciful.
—Luke 6:36

Be Kind to Everyone

Luke 10:25–37

The Thinking Step

- When someone who is not your friend needs help, do you help him or her?
- Would you help someone who is mean to you?

The Listening Step

Jesus told a story to help people know how to be kind. The story was about the good Samaritan. A Jewish man was walking along the road, and bad men hit him and took his money. They left the man hurt and bleeding.

The hurting man saw a priest coming. *He will help me,* the man thought. But the priest kept walking. Then a custodian came walking down the road. *Now I know I will be saved!* the man thought. But the custodian passed by.

The man heard more footsteps. He looked up and saw a Samaritan walking toward him. The man was worried because the Samaritans and the Jews did not like each other. But the Samaritan cleaned the man's cuts and took him to the nearest hotel. "Please take good care of him. I will pay whatever it costs," the Samaritan told the manager.

The Samaritan was a good Samaritan because he helped someone in need even though that person was not his friend.

The Talking Step

- Who was the kind person in the story?
- Who should we try to help?

The Praying Step

- Ask Jesus to show you someone to be kind to this week.
- Ask Jesus to help you be kind to people who are not your friends.

Love your enemies, bless those who curse you, do good to those who hate you.

—Matthew 5:44

Serving One Another

John 13

The Thinking Step

- When work needs to be done, do you do it, or do you expect someone else to do it?

The Listening Step

Jesus was important to the disciples. The disciples knew that they should do what He said. Jesus was their leader. They wanted to follow Him.

One day, just before Jesus was to die on the cross, He told the disciples where to meet Him. It was a room on the second floor. We now call that the Upper Room. When the disciples arrived, something very strange took place. Jesus washed their feet. In those days, feet got very dirty because everyone wore sandals all the time and walked on dusty roads. It was common to wash your feet when you went into someone's house.

But Jesus, God's Son, washed the disciples' feet! The disciples were very surprised. Some of the disciples did not want Him to wash their feet. Peter said to Jesus, "You are not going to wash my feet." But Jesus said, "If I do not wash your feet, you cannot be My disciple." He was trying to teach the disciples a very important lesson. Jesus taught the disciples that it is best to help others.

The Talking Step

- Why did Jesus wash the disciples' feet?
- How should we treat others?

The Praying Step

- Ask Jesus to help you understand how to serve others.
- Ask Jesus to give you chances to help your friends.

For even the Son of Man did not come to be served, but to serve, and to give His life a ransom for many.

—*Mark 10:45*

God Is Getting You Ready

Exodus 2:1–10

The Thinking Step

- Are you learning things every day?
- Do you know God is getting you ready?

The Listening Step

Moses was born a long time ago. When he was born, the Hebrew people were living in Egypt. The Egyptians were afraid there would be too many Hebrew people. So the Egyptians did not want more Hebrew baby boys.

After Moses was born, his mother hid him. She did not want the Egyptians to know he had been born. When she could not hide him in the house anymore, she hid him by the river. Moses' sister watched to be sure that he was safe.

One day the daughter of Pharaoh, the king of Egypt, went down to the river. While she was there, she found Moses. "This is one of the Hebrew babies," she said. Moses' sister heard her and said, "Do you want me to get my mother to take care of the baby for you?" "Yes, please go," Pharaoh's daughter said.

So, Moses' mother took care of him. Then when Moses was old enough, he went to live with Pharaoh's daughter.

God was getting Moses ready during that time. He learned about the Egyptians because he grew up with them. Later Moses would help free the Hebrew people from the Egyptians.

The Talking Step

- Do you think God is getting you ready right now?
- What do you think God is trying to teach you?
- How could you learn more?

The Praying Step

- Thank God for getting you ready to help Him.
- Ask God to help you learn what you should.

Be diligent to present yourself approved to God.
—*2 Timothy 2:15*

God Has a Special Job for You

Exodus 3:1—4:17

The Thinking Step

- Do you think your life is important?
- Do you know God has a special job for you?
- He does!

The Listening Step

Moses had already done a lot in his life. He had done some good things. He had done some bad things.

Moses walked by a mountain one day. He saw something very strange. He saw a bush burning. Nothing happened to the bush. It just burned.

Moses stopped to look at the bush. He wondered why nothing happened to the bush.

Then God spoke to Moses through the bush. "I want you to free My people from Egypt," God told Moses.

"But what if the people will not listen to me? What if they will not believe me?" Moses argued.

"Just tell them I sent you," God said.

"But they still might not believe me," Moses said.

"See that long stick in your hand?" God said. "Throw it on the ground." When Moses threw it on the ground, it turned into a snake. "Now pick it up by its tail," God said. When Moses picked it up, it turned back to a stick.

Moses finally believed God had a special job for him to do. After that, Moses would do God's work.

The Talking Step

- Do you know God has a special job for you?
- What special job do you think He has for you right now?

The Praying Step
- Ask God to show you the special job He has for you.
- Ask God to help you do His special job.

But be doers of the word, and not hearers only.
—*James 1:22*

Little Jobs Become Big Jobs

1 Samuel 1:20–28; 2:18–19; 3:1–10, 19–21

The Thinking Step

- What little jobs does your mom or dad ask you to do?
- Do you get tired of doing these jobs?
- Do you wish you could do something big?

The Listening Step

Hannah was Samuel's mother. She wanted Samuel to serve God. Hannah took him to Eli, the priest. Samuel was going to live with Eli at the temple.

Eli gave Samuel jobs to do. Samuel cleaned. And Samuel made sure the temple looked good.

Eli became older. One night God spoke to Samuel. From then on, Samuel listened for God. He continued to do his work in the temple. As Samuel grew, God had a big job for him to do. When Eli died, Samuel became the new religious leader. He told people what God expected of them.

The Talking Step

- Name some little jobs that God wants you to do.
- Do you think Samuel got tired of doing little jobs, too?

The Praying Step

- Thank God for allowing you to help Him with little jobs.
- Ask God to help you do a good job.
- Ask God to allow you to do bigger jobs for Him, too.

Well done, good and faithful servant.
—*Matthew 25:21*

God Speaks to Me

1 Samuel 3:1–18

The Thinking Step

- Have you ever missed something special because you were not ready?
- Have your mom and dad sometimes wanted you to do something, but they could not find you?
- Sometimes we miss special things when we are not ready.

The Listening Step

Samuel was a little boy. He was staying in the temple with Eli, the priest. One night, while Samuel was in bed, he heard someone call him: "Samuel!" Samuel went into Eli's room. "What do you want?" Samuel asked. "I did not call you," Eli said. "Go back to bed!"

Samuel was confused. He thought he heard Eli call. Then Samuel heard the voice again: "Samuel!" Samuel went to see Eli. "I did not call you," Eli said. "Go back to bed!"

But Samuel heard the voice a third time: "Samuel!" When he went to Eli's room, Eli said, "I am not calling you, Samuel. It must be the Lord. When He calls you again, say 'Speak, Lord, I hear You.'"

Samuel went back to bed. Soon he heard, "Samuel!" Samuel said, "Speak Lord, I hear You." God told Samuel all about a special job He had for him to do. Samuel was ready to listen to God and to do the special job.

The Talking Step

- Have you ever done something to help God?
- What do you think God wants you to do to help Him?
- Are you ready to do what He asks?

The Praying Step
- Tell God you want to be ready to help Him.
- Ask God to tell you how you can help Him.

And Samuel answered, "Speak, for Your servant hears."
—*1 Samuel 3:10*

God Takes Care of Us

1 Kings 17:8–24

The Thinking Step

- Has your mom or dad ever had to give things to help God?
- What happened? Did God take care of your family?
- Does He take care of your family now?

The Listening Step

King Ahab did not love God. God stopped it from raining to punish King Ahab. Because it stopped raining, people did not have much food. Many people were very hungry.

There was a woman living with her son. The woman's husband had died. God asked the woman to give Elijah food to eat. Elijah was God's prophet. He loved God and told people to obey God. But the woman said to Elijah, "I do not have any food to eat. I have only a little flour to make some bread."

Elijah told her, "Fix the food for me, your son, and yourself. God has promised that you will not run out of food."

The woman fixed the food. The food lasted many, many days. Then one day the woman's son got very sick. She said, "This is what I get for helping the prophet Elijah. My son is going to die!" Elijah asked God to save the woman's son, and her son came back to life.

God had taken care of the woman and her son because she helped God.

The Talking Step

- What could you do to help God?
- When you help your friends, are you helping God?
- How will God take care of you?

The Praying Step

- Ask God to give you a chance to help Him.
- Thank God for promising to take care of you.

Then they cried out to the LORD in their trouble,
And He delivered them out of their distresses.
—*Psalm 107:6*

Volunteer for God

Isaiah 6

The Thinking Step

- When your mom and dad ask for someone to help them, do you offer to help? Why?
- How do you think they feel?

The Listening Step

Isaiah loved God. He wanted to make God happy.

One day Isaiah saw God. God was sitting on His throne. God was very powerful. Isaiah was scared. He knew he had done wrong. He knew God was perfect and strong.

God asked Isaiah, "Who should I send? Who will go for Me?" Isaiah did not need to think twice.

"Look at me, Lord," Isaiah called, "I am here. Send me! I will go!"

Isaiah was anxious to volunteer for God. He wanted to be God's helper. He would soon become God's prophet, telling everyone about God.

The Talking Step

- What could you do to be God's helper?
- What could you do to help others?

The Praying Step

- Tell God you want to be His helper.
- Ask God to show you what you can do.

Then I said, "Here am I! Send me."   —*Isaiah 6:8*

Obeying God

Daniel 3

The Thinking Step

- Describe a time your friends disagreed.
- When they disagree, what do you do?
- Do you stand up for one of your friends?

The Listening Step

Shadrach, Meshach, and Abed-Nego were friends. They loved God. They would never do anything to make God sad. God was the only One they were going to worship.

But the king made a rule. Everyone had to bow down and worship him. The king thought he was god! People who did not worship the king would be punished. They would be put into a hot furnace.

What would Shadrach, Meshach, and Abed-Nego do? They loved God. They would rather do what God said even if that meant being put in a hot furnace.

Shadrach, Meshach, and Abed-Nego refused to worship the king. Guess what happened? The king had them thrown into the furnace with fire seven times hotter than usual.

The king was amazed at what he saw. The king said to the people with him, "Not only are the three men still alive, but I see four of them in the furnace. The fourth one looks like an angel!"

God sent an angel to protect Shadrach, Meshach, and Abed-Nego. They were glad they decided to pray to God.

The Talking Step

- Do your friends make fun of you for believing in God?
- What do you do?
- Do you stand up for God?

The Praying Step

- Thank God for taking care of you.
- Ask God to help you obey Him.

He shall call upon Me, and I will answer him;
I will be with him in trouble;
I will deliver him and honor him.
—Psalm 91:15

John Tells About Jesus

John 1:19–36

The Thinking Step

- Have you helped two of your friends become friends with each other?
- It is a nice feeling, is it not?
- John the Baptist did that, too.

The Listening Step

Many people liked John the Baptist. Many people liked to listen to him talk about the coming Christ. Some men liked John so much that they spent every day with him. The men were called his disciples. They followed John the Baptist everywhere. They listened to everything he said.

One day Jesus came to visit John the Baptist. When John saw Jesus coming, he said to everyone, "Look! Here comes the Son of God who saves us from our sins!"

A lot of people started listening to Jesus. Many people followed Jesus instead of John the Baptist. Even some of John's disciples followed Jesus. John the Baptist's other disciples did not like that. They thought the people should listen to John.

But John said, "No, it is okay. That is my job—to tell people about Jesus."

The Talking Step

- Do you think John was sad or happy when people followed Jesus?
- How would you feel if you helped your friends follow Jesus?

The Praying Step

- Think of a friend you could introduce to Jesus.
- Ask God to help you talk to your friend about Jesus.

He must increase, but I must decrease.
—*John 3:30*

Everyone Can Give to God

Luke 21:1–4

The Thinking Step

- Do you take an offering at your church?
- Does your mom or dad give you money to put in the offering?
- God is happy when we give to Him.

The Listening Step

When Jesus lived on earth, there was an offering box at the temple, God's house. People put money in the offering box as their offering to God.

One day Jesus and His disciples were at the temple. They saw people put the money in the offering box. Many people gave a lot of money to God.

Then one woman gave a very small amount to God and put it in the offering box.

Jesus called all the disciples over to Him. "That woman has given more to God with her small offering than all the other people. They gave an offering out of their riches. But she gave an offering when she had very little to give."

The real meaning of the offering is giving to God. It does not matter how much we give.

The Talking Step

- Do you have any money you could give as an offering to God?
- If someone gave you one dollar, what would you do with it?

The Praying Step
- Ask God to teach you the real meaning of an offering.
- Ask God for a chance to give an offering to Him.

Truly I say to you that this poor widow has put in more than all.

—*Luke 21:3*

Final Command

Acts 1:1–11

The Thinking Step

- Do you remember the last thing your mom and dad tell you at night or when they leave the house?
- It is usually something important, is it not?

The Listening Step

Jesus was saying good-bye to His disciples. Everyone was sad. Jesus had changed the lives of the disciples, and they did not want Him to leave. Jesus promised to come back. He also was sending Someone to help the disciples live for Jesus. But they were still sad.

Before Jesus left to go to heaven, He had something very important to tell the disciples. He said, "Go into all the world and tell others about Me." It was one of the last things Jesus told the disciples—to tell others about Him.

The Talking Step

- Why did Jesus tell the disciples to tell others about Him just before He went to heaven?
- How could you tell others about Jesus?

The Praying Step
- Think of someone you could tell about Jesus.
- Ask Jesus to help you talk about Him.

Go therefore and make disciples of all the nations.
—*Matthew 28:19*

Thanking God Comes First

Genesis 8

The Thinking Step

- Describe the last time someone did something really nice for you.
- What was the first thing you did? Why?

The Listening Step

Noah and his family loved God and obeyed Him. God loved Noah and his family too. When it rained for a long time God kept Noah and his family safe inside a big boat, an ark.

It finally stopped raining. Noah wanted to know if it was safe to come out of the ark. So Noah opened a window in the ark. He let a bird out of the ark. The bird found dry land. When the bird did not return to the ark, Noah knew it was safe for them to come out of the ark.

One by one Noah and his family left the ark. They were so happy to see dry land again. They were so happy that God kept them safe. Noah told his family that there was something they should do before they did anything else. They should thank God for keeping them safe.

So Noah and his family met together. They prayed to God and thanked Him for keeping them safe.

The Talking Step

- When was the last time you thanked God for something?
- What could you thank Him for right now?

The Praying Step

- Thank God for something He's done for you lately.
- Thank God for always taking care of you.

It is good to give thanks to the LORD.
—*Psalm 92:1*

God Wants Us to Love Him the Most

Exodus 32

The Thinking Step

- Who is your best friend?
- How would you feel if your best friend liked someone else as much or more than you?
- Would you think you were still best friends?

The Listening Step

Moses was trying to teach the people of Israel about God. He told them they should worship God. He told them they should not worship anyone else.

Some people had seen idols. Idols are statues that people make to worship. Idols are not real. Only God is real.

One day Moses left the people for a little while. He was going to the mountain to pray to God. While Moses was praying, his brother Aaron made an idol of gold. It was a statue of a calf.

Moses finished praying. He came down from the mountain. He saw the people of Israel worshiping the idol! Moses was very upset. He took the idol and threw it in the fire.

"I told you to worship only God!" Moses said. The people learned their lesson. They would worship only God.

The Talking Step

- Sometimes, instead of statues, our idols are other things.
- What things are more important to you than God?
- Are your friends or your toys more important than God?

The Praying Step

- Ask God to help you love only Him.
- Tell God you are sorry for loving other things more than Him.

You shall have no other gods before Me.
—*Exodus 20:3*

Following God's Instructions

Joshua 6

The Thinking Step

- What happens when you do not follow your parents' instructions?
- When an adult puts together a toy and follows the instructions, what happens?

The Listening Step

Jericho was a city. The city had big walls around it.

But the people who lived in Jericho did not like God's people. God's people could not visit Jericho.

God told the people of Israel what to do. They were to march around the city of Jericho once a day for six days. They were to march around the city seven times on the seventh day.

The people of Israel obeyed God's instructions. And on the seventh day some of them marched around the city seven times. Then the priests blew their trumpets, and the men shouted. Guess what happened? The big walls around the city fell down!

The people did what God said to do. God's people followed His instructions.

The Talking Step

- What does God ask you to do?
- Have you followed His instructions?

The Praying Step

- Thank God for giving us the Bible—His instructions.
- Ask God to help you follow His instructions.

You shall walk after the LORD your God and fear Him, and keep His commandments and obey His voice.

—*Deuteronomy 13:4*

Following God's Word

2 Kings 22:1—23:3

The Thinking Step

- What book do you like to read?
- Do you remember what the book says?
- Is that book important to you?

The Listening Step

Do you know someone who is eight years old? Do you think that person could be a king?

Josiah was eight years old. He was the king. He loved God, and he tried to make God happy. When King Josiah was a young man, he asked some men to rebuild the temple. The temple was God's house.

When the men were working, they found God's Word. It had been lost. The people had not been reading God's Word.

They had not been obeying what God said.

King Josiah read God's Word. He read what God wanted the people to do. He also read about God's punishment for disobeying God's commands. The king became very upset because the people had not been following God's Word.

King Josiah read God's Word to the people. He and the people promised to follow God's Word.

The Talking Step

- Name one thing the Bible tells us to do.
- Are you doing it?

The Praying Step
- Ask God to help you obey Him.
- Ask God to teach you what the Bible says.

> But you must continue in the things which you have learned.
>
> *—2 Timothy 3:14*

Doing Hard Things

Esther 7

The Thinking Step

- Think of a time you were on a team for a game or a race. Did your team win?
- What is hard for you to do?
- God asked Esther to do something hard.

The Listening Step

Esther was the queen. She was a Jewish person. Esther loved God.

Haman was one of the king's helpers. Haman did not like the Jewish people. He wanted to kill them.

Mordecai was a leader of the Jewish people. Mordecai sent a note to Queen Esther. He wanted her to talk to the king.

Queen Esther had a problem. The king did not know Esther was Jewish. And no one was allowed to enter the inner court of the palace without the king's permission. The king might want to kill Queen Esther, too.

But Queen Esther knew what she had to do. She sent a note to Mordecai that said, "I will go to the king. And if I die, I die."

Three days later Queen Esther went to see the king. She asked him to come to a banquet. At the banquet, Queen Esther told the king what had happened. She told him that Haman wanted to kill the Jewish people.

The king was very upset. He said Haman should die, instead. Esther was glad she had God on her side.

The Talking Step

- What hard thing did Queen Esther do?
- What happened to Esther?

The Praying Step
- Ask God to help you with hard things.
- Trust God to help you.

> The LORD is on my side;
> I will not fear.
> What can man do to me?
> —*Psalm 118:6*

Choosing to Obey God

Daniel 6

The Thinking Step

- How do you feel when people ask you to do wrong things?
- How do you decide what to do?

The Listening Step

Daniel loved God. He prayed to God every day.

The king made a rule that everyone should pray to him. Anyone praying to God would be put in a den with lions.

What should Daniel do? He wanted to pray to God. But the lions were mean. Daniel did not want to be near the lions.

Daniel chose to obey God. He knew God would keep him safe.

The king found out that Daniel was praying to God. So he made Daniel spend the night with the lions.

The king knew Daniel believed God would keep him safe. The king hoped Daniel would be safe. He said, "May your God keep you safe." He worried all night about Daniel. But when he came to the lions' den, the king found Daniel alive. God kept Daniel safe.

The king made a new rule. All the people were to pray to Daniel's God and worship only Him. Daniel made the right choice!

The Talking Step

- Talk about a time you had to choose between obeying God and doing what your friends wanted you to do.
- Tell what you did and why.

The Praying Step

- Ask God to help you always choose to obey Him.
- Thank Him for being the right choice.

I, the LORD your God, . . . [show] mercy to thousands, to
those who love Me and keep My commandments.

—*Exodus 20:5–6*

Do What Jesus Does

Matthew 3:13–17

The Thinking Step

- Do you have an older brother or sister?
- Do you follow the things he or she does?
- What do you follow?
- Following what someone does is called following the example.

The Listening Step

John the Baptist was telling people about Jesus. John the Baptist baptized those who wanted to lead a new life. He was also telling people that they should ask God to forgive their sins. Sins are the wrong things we do.

One day Jesus came to see John. He asked John to baptize Him, too. John was surprised. Jesus was God's Son. "You should baptize me," John told Jesus.

But Jesus wanted to be baptized to be an example to everyone else. Jesus wanted to be a perfect example for everyone to follow. And He is!

The Talking Step

- How can you follow Jesus' example when you play with your friends?
- How can you follow Jesus' example by what you say, do, and think?

The Praying Step

- Thank Jesus for being the perfect example for us to follow.
- Ask Jesus to help you follow His example.

For I have given you an example, that you should do as I have done to you.

—*John 13:15*

Thinking About Jesus

Matthew 14:25–33

The Thinking Step

- Have you ever tried to walk through your house with your eyes closed?
- Was it a little scary when you bumped into something?

The Listening Step

Peter and the disciples were crossing the lake in a boat. It was very windy. They had to work to keep the boat going straight. As they looked across the water, they saw a Person walking toward their boat. He was walking on the water.

The disciples blinked. They were not sure they believed their own eyes. It was Jesus. Jesus spoke to them, and Peter answered Him.

Then Jesus said to Peter, "Come." Peter got out of the boat. He looked at Jesus and walked on the water. But when Peter noticed what he was doing, he started to sink. Jesus held out His hand and helped Peter up. Peter knew his mistake. He had taken his eyes off Jesus.

The Talking Step

- Why did Peter start to sink?
- What do you ask Jesus to help you with?

The Praying Step

- Ask Jesus to help you.
- Ask Jesus to help you keep thinking about Him.

Looking unto Jesus, the author and finisher of our faith.
—*Hebrews 12:2*

Saying We Are Sorry

Luke 3:1–14; John 1:29–30

The Thinking Step

- Do you remember wrong things you have done?
- Have you asked God to forgive you?
- Do you think He has forgiven you?

The Listening Step

John the Baptist was in the wilderness, outside the city of Jerusalem. He told people about God. He told the people the things they were doing were wrong. John said that God was not happy. God was going to punish them for the wrong things they did—their sins.

The people were worried. "What should we do?" they asked John. "Turn to God and stop sinning!" he told them.

One day Jesus was walking by. John told the people, "Here is the One who can take away your sins!" Many people stopped doing wrong and trusted Jesus.

The Talking Step

- What did John tell the people to do?
- Why do you think they followed Jesus?
- Have you trusted in Jesus to take away your sins?

The Praying Step

- Ask God to forgive you.
- Thank Jesus for taking away your sins.

For all have sinned and fall short of the glory of God.
—*Romans 3:23*

Jesus Is the Most Important

Luke 10:38–42

The Thinking Step

- What is the most important thing in the world to you?
- What do you think about the most?
- What do you spend most of your time doing?

The Listening Step

Mary and Martha were sisters. But they were very different. Martha liked to cook and clean more than Mary did. Mary and Martha were very close friends with Jesus.

One day Jesus went to Mary and Martha's house. Martha was busy fixing the food for them. But Mary did not help her. Mary spent her time talking with Jesus.

Martha became angry. Finally, Martha said to Jesus, "Will You tell Mary to help me? She is making me do all the work!"

"Do not be upset with Mary," Jesus told Martha. "She has decided that spending time with Me is most important to her."

Jesus was most important to Mary. That is why she was talking with Him while Martha was fixing the meal.

The Talking Step

- If you could spend time doing anything, what would it be?
- How could you spend more time with Jesus?

The Praying Step

- Tell Jesus you love Him.
- Ask Him to help you spend more time with Him.

You shall love the LORD your God with all your heart, with all your soul, and with all your strength.

—Deuteronomy 6:5

Showing Jesus You Love Him

Luke 19:1–10

The Thinking Step

- What do you want very much?
- How would you feel if you did not get it?
- What would you do to get it?

The Listening Step

Jesus was coming to Zacchaeus's town. How would you feel if you knew Jesus was coming to your town? Zacchaeus felt the same way. He had to see Jesus.

There was one problem. Wherever Jesus was, people crowded around Him. And Zacchaeus was short. He could not see above the crowd.

Zacchaeus tried to look around the people, but he could not do that. Zacchaeus tried to get to the front of the crowd to see Jesus, but they pushed him back. What could Zacchaeus do? He had to see Jesus.

As Jesus was talking, He looked up. What do you think He saw? He saw Zacchaeus in a tree! Zacchaeus climbed a tree so he could see Jesus. Jesus liked that. He called to Zacchaeus, "Come down from that tree!" Zacchaeus could talk to Jesus now.

The Talking Step

- How hard would you try to see Jesus if you were Zacchaeus?
- What could you do right now to show Jesus you love Him?

The Praying Step
- Tell Jesus you love Him.
- Ask Jesus to help you show love to God and others.

Whoever of you does not forsake all that he has cannot be
My disciple.

—Luke 14:33

Wanting What God Wants

Luke 22:39–46

The Thinking Step

- When you ask your mom and dad for something, are you happy if they want something different?
- Are you interested in what your mom and dad want to do?

The Listening Step

God's plan was for Jesus to die on the cross. Jesus knew He had to die on the cross. That way, we would not have to be punished for our sins. But Jesus did not want to die on the cross.

The night before He died, Jesus prayed to God. He was alone in a special place in the Garden of Gethsemane. "If it is possible," Jesus prayed, "do not let this happen. But most of all, I want whatever You want and whatever You think is best."

There was no other way. Jesus had to die on the cross. And Jesus was happy. What He wanted most of all was to do whatever God wanted.

The Talking Step

- Are you happy if God says no?
- Do you pray for whatever God wants?

The Praying Step

- Ask God to help you want what He wants.
- Ask God to help you understand better what He wants.

Father, if it is Your will, take this cup away from Me;
nevertheless not My will, but Yours, be done.

—*Luke 22:42*

God's House Is Special

John 2:13–17

The Thinking Step

- Think about your church.
- What does the inside of your church look like?
- Why is your church a special place?

The Listening Step

God's house was special to Jesus. Jesus and other people went there to worship God.

But one day when Jesus went to God's house, He saw all sorts of things happening. There were many men in God's house. They were not worshiping God. The men had brought animals into God's house to sell. The men had set up tables and were trying to make money.

Jesus became very angry. He made the men leave God's house. He pushed the animals out. He turned the tables over. "God's house is to be a house of prayer!" Jesus shouted.

God's house is a special place.

The Talking Step

- What would Jesus say if He came to your church?
- How would Jesus want you to behave when you are in God's house?

The Praying Step

- Ask Jesus to help you do the right things in God's house.
- Ask Jesus to be with you as you learn ways to help in church.

My house shall be called a house of prayer for all nations.
—*Mark 11:17*

Tell Others About Jesus

John 9:1–34

The Thinking Step

- Have you ever told a friend about Jesus?
- What do you think you would say to someone about Jesus?

The Listening Step

When Jesus and His disciples were out walking one day, they saw a blind man. Jesus wanted to help the man. He made mud on the ground. He took the mud and spread it on the man's eyes. Jesus said to the man, "Go, wash your eyes in the pool."

The man could see as soon as he washed his eyes. But the Jewish leaders were not happy. People were talking about Jesus rather than talking about them. The Jewish leaders talked to the man's parents. His parents said, "Yes, this is our son who was blind. We do not know how he can see. Ask our son about it."

So the Jewish leaders asked the man who had been blind, "We want to know if Jesus is a good man or not."

The man answered, "You can decide that for yourselves. All I know is that I used to be blind, but now I can see!"

The Talking Step

- What did the man tell people about Jesus?
- What could you tell your friends that Jesus did for you?

The Praying Step

- Ask Jesus to help you know what to tell your friends about Him.
- Ask Jesus to give you a chance to tell others about Him.

One thing I know: that though I was blind, now I see.
—*John 9:25*

Do What Jesus Says

John 21:1–7

The Thinking Step

- When your mom or dad tells you to do something, do you obey right away?
- Do you obey your parents when they ask you to do something that does not make sense?

The Listening Step

One night the disciples decided to go fishing. They were good fishermen. Usually, the disciples caught a lot of fish. But they did not catch anything.

The next morning, Jesus was standing on the beach. But the disciples did not know it was Jesus. Jesus called to them, "Try fishing on the other side of the boat!" The disciples thought that did not make sense.

They had been fishing a long time. They did it anyway. Do you know what happened? They caught so many fish they could not get them all in the boat!

Now the disciples knew who it was. "It is the Lord!" John shouted. The disciples knew that when you do what Jesus says, things work out best.

The Talking Step

- Would you have obeyed Jesus if you were fishing in the boat?
- What would you do if Jesus asked you to do something that did not make sense?

The Praying Step
- Ask Jesus to help you obey Him, even when it is hard.
- Thank Jesus for taking care of you.

If you love Me, keep My commandments.
—John 14:15

Serving God Is Special

Acts 12:25—13:3

The Thinking Step

- What special jobs do you have in your family?
- Why are these jobs special?

The Listening Step

Saul, who was also called Paul, and Barnabas loved Jesus very much. They went to church in the city of Antioch.

But God had a special job for Saul and Barnabas to do. God wanted them to go to many other places and tell people about Jesus. God told the Antioch church to let Saul and Barnabas leave.

They were to go to many other places and do a special job for God.

The people at the church prayed for Saul and Barnabas. They sent them away to do this special job for God.

The Talking Step

- What special job do you think God wants you to do?
- What could you do right now to help God?

The Praying Step

- Tell God you want to help Him.
- Ask God to show you what you can do right now.

> Be doers of the word, and not hearers only, deceiving yourselves.
>
> —*James 1:22*

Praising God When Things Go Wrong

Acts 16:16–34

The Thinking Step

- Do you have days when things go wrong?
- How do you feel when things go wrong?

The Listening Step

Paul and Silas were missionaries. They loved to tell people about Jesus. But some people did not want Paul and Silas to talk about Jesus. Those people made Paul and Silas spend the night in jail.

How would you feel if you were Paul or Silas? Would you be upset?

Paul and Silas were not upset. They were happy! They were telling people about Jesus. Even though Paul and Silas were put in jail, they knew they had a chance to tell people there about Jesus, too.

Do you know what they did? They sang hymns and songs. They praised God. They prayed. Paul and Silas had their own church service.

Even the jail guards heard them. Paul and Silas knew Jesus was taking care of them. They were happy that they could tell people about Jesus.

The Talking Step

- What do you do when things go wrong?
- Have you ever tried thanking and praising God when things go wrong?

The Praying Step

- Ask God to help you thank Him when things are going wrong.
- Thank God for taking care of you.

Rejoice in the Lord always. —*Philippians 4:4*

Obey God Always

Genesis 6

The Thinking Step

- Have you ever been the only one to obey God?
- Did your friends laugh at you?
- How did you feel?

The Listening Step

God was not happy. The world was filled with people doing wrong things. Not many people in the world obeyed God. Noah and his family were the few good people who loved God and obeyed Him.

God decided to make it rain. It was going to rain so much that there would be a flood. But God wanted to keep Noah and his family safe.

God told Noah to build a big boat—an ark. The ark was to be big enough for Noah, his wife, his sons and their wives, and every kind of animal in the world.

When Noah began building the ark, everyone made fun of him. But Noah kept building the ark. He wanted to obey God. Noah knew that he and his family would be safe only if he obeyed God.

The Talking Step

- How do you think Noah felt when people laughed at him?
- Why did he keep obeying God?

The Praying Step
- Ask God to help you keep obeying Him no matter who laughs.
- Ask God to help you know what He wants you to do.

> **Thus Noah did; according to all that God commanded him, so he did.**
>
> **—*Genesis 6:22***

Stepping Out for God

Genesis 12:1–9; 15:5

The Thinking Step

- Have you ever had to move?
- Has your family ever had to do something you were not sure about?
- How did you feel about it?

The Listening Step

Abram and Sarai loved God. They wanted to make God happy.

Abram and Sarai had no children. One day God told Abram to look up in the sky: "See all the stars in the sky." God told Abram, "That is how many children and grandchildren you are going to have. I want you and Sarai to pack all your things and move to a new place. I will show you later where to go."

So Abram and Sarai packed everything they owned and moved away from their home. They did not know where they were going. They trusted God to show them. Abram and Sarai knew that if they did what God wanted, He would care for them.

The Talking Step

- If God asked you to do something difficult, why would you do it?
- Would you trust God to lead you and do what He asked? Why?

The Praying Step

- Ask God to tell you what you should do for Him.
- Ask God to help you trust Him.

In You, O LORD, I put my trust;
Let me never be put to shame.
—*Psalm 71:1*

Be a Peacemaker

Genesis 13

The Thinking Step

- Do you ever have arguments?
- How do you try to settle the argument?

The Listening Step

Abram and his nephew, Lot, shared the same land. Abram had a lot of animals. Lot had many animals, too.

Soon both Abram and Lot had so many animals and men that they were in each other's way. The men who worked for Abram and Lot fought with each other. They all wanted the best land. How would Abram and Lot solve the problem?

Abram and Lot talked about it. Abram told Lot, "There is no need for us to fight. There is plenty of land for both of us. You decide on the land you want, and I will take the rest."

Lot thought that was a good idea. He decided on the best land. Abram took the rest of the land. Abram knew he could give Lot the best land. God had promised to care for Abram and his family.

The Talking Step

- What did Abram do to solve the argument between his men and Lot's men?
- Do you think God was happy about how Abram solved the problem?
- How could you solve your problems the same way?

The Praying Step
- Ask God to help you do the right thing to solve arguments.
- Ask God to help you be a peacemaker.

> Blessed are the peacemakers,
> For they shall be called sons of God.
> —*Matthew 5:9*

Never Doubt God

Exodus 14:1–29

The Thinking Step

- Have you ever felt that God is not listening?
- Have you ever wondered if God would take care of you?

The Listening Step

The Israelites had been servants in Egypt for a long time. God promised the Israelites that they would soon be free. They would live in their own land. God sent Moses to help free the people of Israel.

The king of Egypt let the Israelites go. But soon the army of Egypt came after them. The people of Israel went faster and faster, but the Egyptians were catching up to them.

Then the Israelites saw the Red Sea right in front of them. They were trapped!

The Egyptian army was getting closer and closer. And the people of Israel were getting angry. "Why did God bring us out here to die?" they cried. "We were better off as servants in Egypt!"

But God was true to His word. Moses put his long stick over the water. The Red Sea divided. There was a dry pathway right in the middle. The people of Israel walked through the middle of the sea and were safe. God protected them and brought them to freedom.

The Talking Step

- Talk about a time you wondered if God was going to take care of you. Did He?
- What should we do when we doubt if God will keep His promises?

The Praying Step
- Thank God for always keeping His promises and taking care of us.
- Ask God to help you trust Him.

For with God nothing will be impossible.
—*Luke 1:37*

Be Loyal to God

Ruth 1—4

The Thinking Step

- Do you have special jobs to do in your home?
- Do you ever get tired of doing them?
- What do your parents tell you when you complain about your jobs?

The Listening Step

Naomi and her husband had two sons. But Naomi's husband died. Her two sons married Ruth and Orpah. Then Naomi's sons died, too. Naomi was left with Orpah and Ruth.

One day Naomi said to Orpah and Ruth, "Please go back home now to your mothers. You were good wives to my sons. May God bless you." Orpah and Ruth cried. They loved Naomi. They did not want to leave her.

Orpah cried and kissed Naomi. Orpah went home to live with her mother. But Ruth would not leave.

Naomi and Ruth stayed together. They moved to another place. There they met a man named Boaz.

Boaz had a lot of land. So Ruth gathered grain from Boaz's fields.

Soon Ruth and Boaz married. They had a child. Their child became grandfather of David, who fought Goliath. David became king and was a special man for God.

Ruth stayed with Naomi. She was loyal to God. God blessed her for it and gave her a special son.

The Talking Step

- Name something special God has asked you to do.
- What do you think you should do if it becomes difficult?
- Would God want you to continue doing what He has asked you to do?

The Praying Step

- Ask God to let you know what you should do.
- Ask God to help you continue doing what He wants.

> Blessed are those who keep His testimonies,
> Who seek Him with the whole heart!
> —*Psalm 119:2*

Giving Back to God

1 Samuel 1:24–28

The Thinking Step

- Why do you like getting presents?
- Have you received such a wonderful present that you wanted to give something back in return?
- That is how Hannah felt!

The Listening Step

Hannah loved her baby. Her baby's name was Samuel.

Hannah knew God had given her the baby. She wanted to give God a present, too. But what could she give God? He had everything!

Hannah thought and thought. Finally, she had the perfect present.

Hannah took Samuel to Eli, the priest. She told Eli, "This is Samuel. He was a gift to me from God. Now I want to give him back to God. He will serve God with all his heart."

The Talking Step

- Name something special you have given God.
- What could you give Him today?
- How does God feel when we give Him something special?

The Praying Step
- Tell God you love Him.
- Ask Him to help you remember to give Him something special.

It is more blessed to give than to receive.

—Acts 20:35

Be Happy for Your Friends

1 Samuel 18:1–16

The Thinking Step

- Describe a time you wanted something very much.
- How would you have felt if one of your friends got it instead of you?
- Would that person have stayed your friend? Why or why not?

The Listening Step

Saul was the king of Israel. King Saul was very important. Many people followed him. Everyone did whatever King Saul told them to do.

But David was very well liked too. Some people liked David better than they liked King Saul.

This made King Saul very upset. He was worried that these people would want David to be king instead of him. So Saul did not like David.

One day they had a parade for King Saul. But many people cheered louder for David than for the king. "I'm going to keep my eye on David," thought Saul, "I'm worried about him."

King Saul should have been happy that David was so well liked. But instead he was angry. Saul wanted everyone to only like him, not David.

The Talking Step

- How do you think God wants you to act when your friends do things well? Why?

The Praying Step

- Ask God to help you be happy when your friends do well.
- Ask God to help you make Him happy all the time.

If one member is honored, all the members rejoice with it.
—*1 Corinthians 12:26*

Let God Do It His Way

1 Samuel 26

The Thinking Step

- Have you ever tried to do something and found that someone else had a better way to do it?

The Listening Step

King Saul did not like David. The king thought that too many people liked David. King Saul was trying to kill David. David was scared. He was running away from the king.

One night while David was trying to find a safe place to hide, he found King Saul. The king was asleep.

David's friend called him, "David, it is King Saul! Let me kill him now!"

David did not think he or his friend should kill King Saul. God made Saul king. To kill the king would be to fight against God. And David did not want to do that.

Later, David would be king. God would make him king—His way.

The Talking Step

- What was King Saul trying to do to David? Why?
- How did God take care of David?

The Praying Step

- Talk to God about a special problem.
- Ask God to help you be patient.
- Ask God to help you trust Him.

> Commit your way to the LORD,
> Trust also in Him,
> And He shall bring it to pass.
> —*Psalm 37:5*

Stay Close to God

1 Kings 2:1–4

The Thinking Step

- If your parents were only able to tell you one thing, what would it be?
- What is the most important lesson your parents or teacher would want you to know?

The Listening Step

King David was a good king. He had been king for a long time. Now it was time for David's son, Solomon, to be king. King David wanted his son to be a good king. He wanted to tell Solomon everything he needed to know.

"Do what God tells you to do," King David told Solomon. "Be sure to always obey Him. Follow whatever God says in the Law of Moses. If you do, you will be a good king."

Then Solomon became king. King Solomon was a wise king. He listened to his father and tried to obey God.

The Talking Step

- Why did King David choose obeying God as his final instruction for Solomon?
- What will happen to you if you obey God your entire life?

The Praying Step

- Tell God you want to obey Him.
- Ask God to help you always do what He says.

And keep the charge of the LORD your God: to walk in His ways, to keep His statutes, His commandments.

—*1 Kings 2:3*

Your Mind Matters

1 Kings 3:1–15

The Thinking Step

- If your mom or dad said you could have whatever you wanted, what would it be?
- Are you sure?

The Listening Step

Solomon was David's son. Solomon was a good king. He loved God.

One day God said to Solomon, "What do you want Me to give you?" It was a hard question. God could give Solomon whatever he wanted. Should Solomon ask for happiness? Should he ask for money? Should he ask for a big house and lots of friends?

Solomon thought for a long time. Then he said to God, "There is one thing I need more than any other. I am young. Everyone comes to me asking for help, and I do not know what to do. I would like a mind able to understand and know what to do."

God was very pleased. Solomon had asked for the right thing. He wanted to help others. So God told Solomon, "Not only will I give you an understanding mind, I will also give you money and happiness and a beautiful home!"

Solomon did the right thing. He asked for a mind to understand. Even today we remember Solomon for his wisdom.

The Talking Step

- Who gave you your mind?
- How do you think you could have an understanding mind?

The Praying Step

- Ask God to give you a wise mind.
- Ask God to help you use your mind.
- Thank God for helping you think of what is best for yourself and others.

> **For as he thinks in his heart, so is he.**
> **—Proverbs 23:7**

Do Not Give Up

1 Kings 19:1–18

The Thinking Step

- Have you ever had trouble getting something done?
- Do you sometimes feel like giving up? Why?
- Elijah felt like giving up, too.

The Listening Step

Elijah was God's prophet. Elijah loved God. He wanted to tell people about God. He told people they should obey God. Many people did not like to hear what he told them. The queen, Jezebel, sent a note to Elijah. The note said, "You will die!"

Elijah was scared. He thought, *What is the use? I have tried to tell people to obey God. But I am the only one who believes in God.*

So Elijah ran away. He found a cave and spent the night in it. God knew where Elijah went. "What are you doing here?" God asked Elijah.

"I have tried telling people about You," Elijah told God. "And I am the only one left who loves You."

God told Elijah to keep following Him: "Seven thousand people still love Me."

Elijah learned that things were better than he thought.

The Talking Step

- God wants us to ask Him for help when we feel like giving up.
- Have you ever felt like Elijah and wanted to give up?

The Praying Step
- Ask God to help you keep trying.
- Thank God for always helping you.

Rest in the LORD, and wait patiently for Him.
—*Psalm 37:7*

Trust God

Job 1—3; 42:10

The Thinking Step

- Have you ever had a really bad day?
- What do you do when things seem to go wrong?

The Listening Step

Job loved God. He always thanked God for everything. Job made God happy. Job had many things. He had thousands of sheep and many other animals. He also had a lot of land. Job and his wife had ten children. They were very happy.

One day Job's life changed. A man who worked for Job came to him and said, "We were working in the field. Men attacked us and took away the animals." Then another man showed up. "What happened?" Job asked. "All the sheep caught on fire and died!" the man said.

A short time later, a man came to tell Job some more news. "All your children were together," the man said. "The wind blew the house down, and they all died!"

Even after those terrible things happened, Job loved God. God gave Job much more in return for all he lost.

The Talking Step

- Do you trust God to take care of you when you have a hard day?
- Do you think God will take care of you like He took care of Job?

The Praying Step

- Thank God for taking care of you.
- Ask God to help you trust Him like Job did, no matter how bad things become.

The God of my strength, in whom I will trust.
—*2 Samuel 22:3*

God Knows What You Do

Jonah 1—3

The Thinking Step

- When your parent or teacher is not watching, do you try to get away with doing wrong things?
- Do you wonder how people find out what you did?
- Do you think God knows what you do?

The Listening Step

Jonah did not like the people in Nineveh. But God wanted Jonah to tell them about God. Jonah acted like he was going to obey, but he disobeyed instead.

Jonah went to the sea. He saw the boat going to Nineveh.

Jonah did not get on the boat to Nineveh. Jonah got on a boat going in the other direction. He thought he had fooled God. But God knew what Jonah did. God sent a big storm. The men on the boat were scared. They started to throw everything out of the boat. The storm was still too strong.

Jonah knew God had sent the storm because he disobeyed. He told the men on the boat, "God sent this bad storm because I disobeyed Him. Throw me into the water, and you will be safe." So they threw Jonah into the water. Guess what happened? The storm stopped.

Then a big fish swallowed Jonah. He spent three days inside the fish. While he was in the fish, Jonah talked to God. He promised to obey God. When Jonah got out of the fish, he went straight to Nineveh to preach. Jonah knew God was watching!

The Talking Step

- Do you think Jonah would have disobeyed if he had known God was watching?
- What would you have done differently if you had known God was watching you?
- How will you act differently tomorrow knowing God is watching you?

The Praying Step

- Thank God for caring enough about you to watch you all the time.
- Ask God to help you obey all the time.

You know my sitting down and my rising up;
You understand my thought afar off.
—*Psalm 139:2*

The Bible Helps You

Matthew 4:1–11

The Thinking Step

- Do you sometimes do wrong things even when you try to be good?
- Do you know the best way to be good?

The Listening Step

Jesus was very tired. He was also very hungry. He had been in the wilderness a long time. Jesus wanted to be good. But Satan tried to make Jesus do something wrong. Satan knew Jesus was hungry. So he told Jesus to make the stones on the ground into bread. Jesus said, "The Bible says, 'Man shall not live by bread alone.'"

Then Satan took Jesus to the top of God's house and said, "Jump off. Will not God take care of You?" Jesus said, "The Bible says, 'You shall not tempt God.'"

Then Satan said, "If You will worship me, I will give You power over the entire world." Jesus said, "The Bible says, 'You shall worship only the LORD God.'"

So Satan left. Jesus used God's Word every time. God's Word helped Him be good.

The Talking Step

- What did Jesus do every time Satan tempted Him to do wrong?
- What can help you obey God?
- How can the Bible help you be good?

The Praying Step

- Ask God to help you know the Bible.
- Ask God to help you be good.

All Scripture is given by inspiration of God.
—2 Timothy 3:16

Spend Time with God

Luke 2:41–52

The Thinking Step

- What do you want to do when you meet a new friend?
- How do you get to know someone better?

The Listening Step

Jesus was twelve years old. His parents took Him to the big city of Jerusalem. It was a special time in Jerusalem. A lot of people were in the city. Jesus and His parents walked around the big city. They saw many interesting things.

Many people traveled home together. Jesus' parents went with them. They thought Jesus was in the group. But Jesus' parents did not see Him.

They kept looking for Jesus. Still they did not see Him. Soon Jesus' parents started to worry. They walked through the crowd. "Have you seen Jesus?" they asked. No one had seen Him.

Jesus' parents decided He must be in Jerusalem. So they went back there. His parents looked up and down the streets. They looked in buildings. And they finally found Jesus. Do you know where? In the temple. When Jesus' parents walked in, they saw all the religious teachers sitting with Him. Jesus was asking questions and talking about God.

Jesus' parents were upset. "We were worried about You," they said. "Why?" asked Jesus. "Did you not know that I would be in God's house?" Most of all Jesus wanted to spend time with God.

The Talking Step

- Why was Jesus in the temple?
- What happens when we spend time with God?

The Praying Step

- Ask God to help you spend more time with Him.
- Ask God to teach you more about Him.

But his delight is in the law of the LORD,
And in His law he meditates day and night.
—Psalm 1:2

Always Thank God

Luke 17:11–19

The Thinking Step

- Do you thank your mom and dad when they do nice things for you?
- Do you thank people for the presents they give you?

The Listening Step

One day Jesus saw some lepers. Lepers had a disease. Other people did not want to be near lepers because they did not want to catch the disease, too.

But Jesus wanted to help the lepers and make them well. Jesus rubbed mud on them. The ten lepers ran to wash off the mud. When they did, the lepers were not sick anymore.

Jesus said, "Go, show yourselves to the priests." On their way, the lepers looked at each other. They saw that they were not sick anymore.

Nine of the ten lepers were so excited that they ran to tell their friends. Do you know what the other leper did? He went back to thank Jesus for making him well. Jesus liked that very much.

The Talking Step

- How do you feel when someone thanks you for something?
- How do you think your mom and dad feel when you say thanks?
- How do you think God feels when you thank Him for what He has done?
- How do you think God feels when you do not thank Him?

The Praying Step
- What can you thank God for today?
- Thank Him for all He has done for you.
- Thank Him for loving you and taking care of you.

Oh, give thanks to the LORD, for He is good!
—*Psalm 118:1*

You Cannot Say No to God

Acts 9:1–20

The Thinking Step

- Have you ever met people who would not take no for an answer?
- Do they usually get what they want?
- What do they do if you tell them no?

The Listening Step

Saul did not like Jesus. He did not even like people who believed in Jesus. Saul thought that Jesus' followers were hurting God. Saul tried to stop the believers of Jesus.

One day Saul and his friends were traveling. A bright light shone from heaven. Saul fell to the ground. Then Jesus spoke to Saul. "Why are you hurting Me?" Jesus asked. Saul was confused. "Who are You, Lord?" Saul wanted to know. "I am Jesus, whom you are hurting," Jesus said.

Saul understood. He knew Jesus was God's Son. He would follow Jesus. His name was later changed to Paul.

The Talking Step

- Have you ever tried saying no to God?
- What happened?

The Praying Step

- Tell God you want to obey Him.
- Ask Him to help you let Him have His way.

As for God, His way is perfect. —*Psalm 18:30*

God Keeps His Promise

Genesis 18:1–15; 21

The Thinking Step

- Can you think of something that someone promised you?
- Did you wonder if the promise would be kept?
- Did you stop hoping?

The Listening Step

God promised Abraham that he and his wife, Sarah, would have a son. In fact, God told Abraham he would have as many members of his family as there are stars in the sky.

But Abraham and Sarah did not have any sons. They did not have any children. Abraham told Sarah about the promise.

She said, "How can that be? I am too old to have children!"

As the years went by, Abraham and Sarah began to doubt whether God would give them children. But one day, Sarah had a baby. They named their baby boy Isaac. God was faithful. He kept His promise.

The Talking Step

- Why do you think God keeps His promises?
- Have you ever gotten tired of waiting for God? When was that?
- Sometimes it is hard to keep waiting, but God keeps His promises.

The Praying Step

- Think of what God has promised you.
- Ask God to help you trust Him.
- Thank God for keeping His promises to you.

He who calls you is faithful, who also will do it.
—*1 Thessalonians 5:24*

God Makes Good Out of Bad

Genesis 37:12–36; 40:1–19; 41:9–41

The Thinking Step

- What is a bad day?   • How do you feel on a bad day?
- Do you think that any good can come out of days like that?

The Listening Step

Joseph had many brothers. His older brothers did not like him. They were mean to him.

Joseph's brothers played a trick on him. They sold him to a man who lived far away. Joseph would be his slave and do whatever the man wanted. That man sold Joseph to another man, who lived in Egypt. Joseph was put in charge of his master's house.

One day Joseph was blamed for something he did not do. His master put him in jail. Joseph met two men in jail. He told the two men what would happen to them. God told him what to tell the men.

Later, one of the men told the king of Egypt about Joseph. Joseph told the king that Egypt would have much food. But then, he said, there would be many years with little food. Joseph also told the king what to do about it.

What do you think happened to Joseph? The king put him in charge of the food for the whole country. The king told his helpers to do whatever Joseph asked them to do. God made good out of the bad that happened to Joseph.

The Talking Step

- What bad things happened to Joseph?
- What good things did God have happen to Joseph?
- Name a time in which a bad thing happened to you or your family that turned out to be good.

The Praying Step

- Thank God for caring for you.
- Ask God to help you trust Him to make things good even if they seem bad.

And we know that all things work together for good to those who love God, to those who are the called according to His purpose.

—Romans 8:28

God Does Not Take No for an Answer

Exodus 5—13

The Thinking Step

- Would you ever say no to God?
- Have you ever said no to God?
- When a person says no to God, what do you think will happen?

The Listening Step

God's people, the Hebrews, had been servants in Egypt a long time. But God did not want His people to be servants anymore. God sent Moses to free them.

Moses went to talk to Pharaoh, the king of Egypt. "God says, 'Let My people go!'" said Moses. Pharaoh said, "No, I will not."

"Then terrible things will happen to Egypt," said Moses, "until you do what God wants." Pharaoh still would not obey God.

God made many bad things happen in Egypt. Each time Moses said to Pharaoh, "Let God's people go!" And each time Pharaoh said, "No, I will not." Big hailstones fell, cattle died, crops died, and people died. Finally, Pharaoh agreed to let God's people go.

The Talking Step

- Do you think it would have been easier for Pharaoh to obey right away?
- Have you ever not obeyed God but wished you had?

The Praying Step
- Ask God to forgive you for not obeying Him.
- Ask God to help you obey Him in all things.

As I live, says the LORD,
Every knee shall bow to Me,
And every tongue shall confess to God.
—Romans 14:11

Make Sure God Is on Your Side

Judges 6:36–40

The Thinking Step

- Describe a time someone offered to help you do something.
- Could you have done it without their help?
- How did you know they would help you?

The Listening Step

Gideon was a leader in Israel. Many people looked to him for help. But Gideon knew he couldn't lead the people by himself. He needed God's help. But would God help him?

Gideon had to know for sure, so he talked to God about it. "Are You going to help me?" Gideon asked God. Gideon had an idea. "I will put out a piece of wool tonight," Gideon said to God. "If the wool is wet tomorrow but the ground is dry, then I will know You are going to help me."

So Gideon put the wool out that night. When he woke up in the morning he went out to see what happened. The ground was dry. But the piece of wool was soaking wet. He squeezed enough water out of the wool to fill a bowl!

But Gideon had to be sure. "Let me ask one more thing. I am going to put another piece of wool out tonight. This time let the wool be dry and let the ground be wet," he said.

So Gideon put the wool out again. The next morning he saw that the ground was very wet. But the piece of wool was dry.

Now Gideon knew for sure. God would help him be a great leader.

The Talking Step

- How do you know God will help you?
- What are special things in which you want God's help?

The Praying Step

- Tell God you want His help in something special.
- Ask God to show you He will help you.

The LORD is my rock and my fortress and my deliverer.
—*Psalm 18:2*

God Overcomes Everything

1 Samuel 17

The Thinking Step

- Describe a time you were scared.
- Were you afraid of someone or something?

The Listening Step

David was a young boy. One day David's father asked him to take food to his brothers. His brothers were soldiers in the armies of Israel.

When David arrived, he saw a giant named Goliath. Goliath was as tall as you and two of your friends put together! Goliath was making fun of David's brothers and everyone else in the armies of Israel. "What is the matter? Are you all afraid of me?" Goliath yelled.

David trusted in God. He said he would fight the giant. Since no one else was willing to face Goliath, the commander agreed. He put armor on David, but it was so big it fell off.

So David went out to face the giant with only his slingshot. But David trusted in God. He calmly picked five stones and put one in his sling. David shot the stone at Goliath. With one shot, Goliath fell. God had overcome the giant!

The Talking Step

- Do you think David was scared?
- What problems can you trust God to overcome?

The Praying Step

• Ask God to help you trust Him.

The Lord reigns;
Let the earth rejoice.
—Psalm 97:1

God Always Wins

1 Kings 18

The Thinking Step

- Do you know someone who always wins?
- There is Someone else who always wins.

The Listening Step

Elijah was God's prophet. He told the people what God wanted them to know.

Some people did not like that. Some people liked to worship idols. Idols are make-believe gods made by people.

Elijah wanted to show everyone that the Lord was the only true God. He wanted everyone to believe in God. Elijah told all the people to meet him. He wanted to talk to those who worshiped Baal, too.

"It is time you decided," Elijah said. "If Baal is God, worship him. If the Lord is God, worship Him."

They built two altars: one for Baal and one for the Lord. But they did not build a fire. The believers of Baal prayed to him. They wanted him to start a fire in the altar. They prayed for a long time.

Elijah made fun of the people praying to Baal: "You better call louder! Maybe he cannot hear you!"

Finally, the people gave up. They stopped praying to Baal.

Then it was the Lord's turn. Elijah had men pour water all over the altar. They poured water on the wood, too.

Elijah prayed, "O Lord, I know You are the only true God. Bring fire upon this altar. Show these people that You are the only true God!" With that, the wood and even the stones of the altar burst into flames and burned up. Everyone knew that the Lord was the only true God!

The Talking Step

- Name a problem you have had.
- How can God help you defeat that problem?

The Praying Step

- Ask God to help you win over the problems you have.
- Ask God to help you do what He wants.

Yet in all these things we are more than conquerors through Him who loved us.

—Romans 8:37

Jesus Is King

Matthew 21:1–9

The Thinking Step

- Have you ever seen a king on television or read about a king in a book?
- Does everyone do what a king says? Why?

The Listening Step

Jesus was near Jerusalem. The people were excited. They were waiting for Him.

Soon Jesus entered Jerusalem. He was riding a donkey. The people started cheering. "Hosanna! Blessed is He who comes in the name of the Lord!" they shouted. They placed palm branches on the road for Him to ride over.

The people treated Jesus as their King. The people were glad they could see Him.

The Talking Step

- What would you do if you saw a king?
- What would you do if you saw Jesus right now?
- What does it mean that Jesus is King?

The Praying Step
- Thank Jesus that He is King.
- Ask Jesus to take care of you.

That at the name of Jesus every knee should bow, of those in heaven, and of those on earth, and of those under the earth.

—*Philippians 2:10*

God Is in Charge of Everything

John 18:1—19:16

The Thinking Step

- What does it mean to be in charge of something?

The Listening Step

Jesus is God's Son. Jesus did what God wanted. God wanted Jesus to die on the cross. That was the only way we could be forgiven and go to heaven.

Pilate was in charge of the people in Jerusalem. He was supposed to make important decisions for the people who lived there.

Some of the leaders were not happy because Jesus told the people to follow Him. The leaders sent men to arrest Jesus late at night. They thought they could solve the problem themselves.

After the men arrested Jesus, they took Him to Pilate. Pilate wanted to talk to Jesus. But Jesus would not answer his questions.

"Why will You not answer me?" Pilate asked. "Do You not know that I have the power to let You live or not?"

"The only power you have is what My Father in heaven has given you," Jesus said.

God's plan was for Jesus to die for us on the cross. And that is exactly what happened. God was in charge all along.

The Talking Step

- How does it make you feel to know God is in charge of everything in your life?
- How does it help when you have a hard day?

The Praying Step
- Thank God for being in charge.
- Ask God to help you let Him be in charge of your life.

The earth is the LORD's, and all its fullness,
The world and those who dwell therein.
—Psalm 24:1

God Does Things Right

Acts 8:1—9:2

The Thinking Step

- Did you ever do something wrong and wish someone else had done it for you?
- Do you know people who always seem to do things right?

The Listening Step

Saul did not like the church. He thought Christians should not believe in Jesus. Saul was trying to hurt the church and the Christians. He thought he was helping God.

The Christians were in Jerusalem. Every day more and more people believed in Jesus. Each week more people joined the church. That made Saul unhappy. He put many Christians in jail. The Christians were scared. Many of them ran away from Jerusalem.

Christians moved to many places. Soon there were churches in each place and many more Christians, too. God helped the church grow.

The Talking Step

- Do you think the Christians thought God was in charge when they were being hurt?
- Are there times when you wonder if God is doing the right thing?
- Name a time when God did the right thing.

The Praying Step
- Thank God for always doing the right thing.
- Ask God to help you trust Him.

For the word of the LORD is right.
—*Psalm 33:4*

Jesus Can Make a Difference

Acts 9:10–31

The Thinking Step

- Are there some people you have trouble getting along with?
- Do you think they can ever change?
- Do you think Jesus can help them change?

The Listening Step

Saul scared the Christians. He did not like them. He was trying to hurt them. The Christians ran away from Jerusalem to be safe from Saul.

Then one day Saul met Jesus. He learned that Jesus was God's Son. Saul also learned that Jesus loved him.

What do you think the Christians thought when they saw Saul? They were scared. Saul told them that he loved Jesus, too.

The Christians were not sure. But they learned to trust Saul. Jesus made a difference in his life.

The Talking Step

- Do you think Jesus can change a person's life?
- How do people who know Jesus act differently?

The Praying Step
- Pray for people who need Jesus to help them.
- Ask Jesus to help you tell others about Him.

Therefore, if anyone is in Christ, he is a new creation;
old things have passed away; behold, all things have
become new.

—*2 Corinthians 5:17*